Life After Death

Life After Death
Where do I go now

Peggy Ricciuto

gatekeeper press™
Columbus, Ohio

The views and opinions expressed in this book are solely those of the author and do not reflect the views or opinions of Gatekeeper Press. Gatekeeper Press is not to be held responsible for and expressly disclaims responsibility of the content herein.

Life After Death: Where do I go now

Published by Gatekeeper Press
2167 Stringtown Rd, Suite 109
Columbus, OH 43123-2989
www.GatekeeperPress.com

Copyright © 2021 by Peggy Ricciuto
All rights reserved. Neither this book, nor any parts within it may be sold or reproduced in any form or by any electronic or mechanical means, including information storage and retrieval systems, without permission in writing from the author. The only exception is by a reviewer, who may quote short excerpts in a review.

The cover design, interior formatting, typesetting, and editorial work for this book are entirely the product of the author. Gatekeeper Press did not participate in and is not responsible for any aspect of these elements.

Library of Congress Control Number: 2021931739

ISBN (paperback): 9781662910043
eISBN: 9781662910050

Contents

Foreword	vii
Prologue	ix
Chapter 1 Unexpected Death	1
Part A — Prior Planning	1
Part B — Can We Expect the Unexpected When it Comes to Death?	3
Chapter 2 Expected Death	5
A — Death Is No Respecter of Persons or Plans	5
B — Not Related by Blood or Marriage	7
Chapter 3 Planning Ahead	9
A — Is There Such a Thing as Too Much Planning?	9
B — Recording Your Wishes	12
C — Keep It Simple	12
Chapter 4 Where Do I Start?	15
A. Wills	15
B. Living will	16
C. Trusts	17
D. Insurance	18
(1) Life insurance	18
(2) Credit cards/financial institutions/mortgage insurance	18
(3) Burial insurance	19

E. Financial documents	19
F. Funeral arrangements	20
G. Whom to notify	20
H. Disposition of possessions	21
(1) Joint accounts	21
(2) Vehicles (to include boats, RV's, motorcycles, etc.)	22
(3) Real estate	22
Chapter 5 Things To Consider During Planning Or Upon Death	25
A. Obituary	25
B. Social Security	25
C. Credit reporting agencies	26
D. Miscellaneous information	26
E. Death certificates	27
F. Other considerations	28
Chapter 6 Getting Through The Inevitable	29
Chapter 7 Do I Need A Lawyer?	31
Chapter 8 Special Circumstances	33
Chapter 9 One Last Thing: A Personal Letter	35
Chapter 10 The Grieving Process	37
Chapter 11 The Final Chapter	43
Chapter 12 Recap	45
Chapter 13 Reflections	51
Addendum	53

Foreword

I have always wanted to write a book, but nothing came to me in the way of inspiration until I started working with veterans as a counselor. One day it struck me that there are many people who are unprepared to face life after a death and have no idea how to handle the aftermath of a loved one's death. I found there are hundreds of books and websites that provide information, but I felt it was important to put some of this information in one place, in a handbook. With encouragement from my soul mate, Chip, I launched on the daunting project of this book. If it helps one widow, one widower, or anyone who had to face a death or an impending death, then I have accomplished my task. To the survivors, remember, life will go on, and hopefully this book will help you find life after death.

I would like to thank my friend, C.J. Geotis for reading my rough drafts and providing guidance along the way.

DISCLAIMER: This book is not intended to provide any financial, tax or legal advice. For this type of advice, you should seek assistance from a qualified individual.

Prologue

This is not a book about reincarnation. It is about preparing you and your loved ones for the inevitable — DEATH. It is about the importance of preparing yourself and others for life before and after the death of a loved one. Even more importantly, it is about preparing for your own death.

Shakespeare addressed the subject of inevitable death in *Julius Caesar*: "Of all the wonders that I yet have heard, it seems to me most strange, that man should fear, seeing that death, a necessary end, will come when it will come."

What do we know about death? We know that it is inevitable. But although death is inevitable, most people are not prepared for death, not someone else's and definitely not their own. Death can be an unexpected event, or it can be a long, agonizing ordeal both for the person going through the process and for those on the sidelines watching hopelessly. There is no single checklist a spouse/survivor can use because each death and each estate will be as different as each individual. We know that death will come when it will come, as Shakespeare said.

Death obviously affects only those left behind. Some of us have experienced the painful loss of a loved one. It does not matter whether it is a parent, sibling, spouse, child, or friend; the pain is not lessened. Besides the obvious mental drain, the aftermath of a death means a person can be left wondering what to do. Many of us are not prepared to deal with all the details that must be taken care of, either to prepare for an expected death or in the event of an unexpected death.

Whether you are the executor of a will, a family member, or even a friend, you may be the one who has the responsibility to deal with final burial arrangements as well as disposition of the deceased's estate.

People die every day, and not all are mourned or even missed, but no matter what the circumstances, the death of one person usually has an effect on someone else.

Millions of people each year must face the questions: "What do I do when a loved one dies, or what will my loved ones do when I die?" First, let us think about what you can do before death. This means making plans for your own death as well as talking with your loved ones about their wishes. As ominous as this may sound, we must admit we are not immortal and someday our time will come. Many people feel they can put these preparations off until they are in their "golden" or "twilight" years. Not so. Every person, when they become an adult should make some preparations, whether they write simple, informal instructions or prepare the more formal will and other legal documents. This becomes even more important if you marry or have children. Even after preparing these documents, you must make sure they are reviewed and updated periodically or as changes happen. Let us look at some different scenarios, and maybe you can identify yourself in one or more of them.

Chapter 1
Unexpected Death

Part A — Prior Planning

Rose became an unexpected widow at 43. She was stunned because Tom, at 49, had a massive heart attack and died. They had never talked about the "what ifs" and "if something happens to me," so Rose was at a loss about where to start or what to do. She was in a daze, too shocked to face the reality of the situation. Well-meaning friends and relatives were there right after the funeral, and then she was left alone to deal with what to do next. She had no idea where to turn; Tom had always taken care of everything. Luckily, a friend, who had gone through the death of a loved one, provided her with a list of things she needed to accomplish.

The first thing Rose had to face was the funeral itself. Do I bury Tom, or do I cremate him? What type of casket and service should I choose if I bury him? What do I do with the ashes if I cremate him? They had never talked about this because "death" was a subject that did not come up. In Rose's hometown, there were several funeral homes, and she finally selected one based on the recommendation of her friend. It was a good choice, and the funeral home turned out to be a reputable one. The funeral director guided Rose through the selection of a casket, as she decided since all his family had been buried, she would continue with that tradition. In addition, she was able to determine if she needed a vault, the type of headstone acceptable to the cemetery, whether to have a viewing, what type of service to have, what music to be played, whether to have a celebration of his life or if a wake or some other type of religious ceremony was appropriate, how to select clothing for him to be buried in, how to select pallbearers, and many other details involved in a funeral. For this, the funeral director was the "go-to" guy because this was his profession, and he knew what needed to be done.

But let us back up a little; what if Rose and Tom had already discussed death and knew what each other wanted? What if they had already purchased burial/funeral insurance? What if they already had a plot paid for and had put in writing exactly what they wanted, down to the type of ceremony and the music to be played? How much simpler would this have been and how much stress could have been eliminated for Rose? We cannot all be the perfect planners, but knowing that at some time in our lives, we will face death and a decision about a loved one's death, it seems only logical we should do our planning while we are alive.

Of course, once the funeral is over, that is not the end of what needs to be done. Rose needed to find out about bank accounts, credit cards, vehicle registration, mortgage insurance, mortgage payments, life insurance, organization memberships, magazine subscriptions, prescription medications, doctors' appointments, etc. She had to find out what her financial situation would be since Tom was the "breadwinner." For these questions and others, she had to determine if talking with her banker, her broker, or her lawyer was the best course of action or if she needed to talk with all three. In the end, she had to determine who handled what to determine where she stood financially. Did Tom plan for these contingencies by buying life insurance, having a will or trust established, or having joint accounts, or did he think he was too young to do all these things? Rose would only learn this as she delved into each of these areas. It seemed an insurmountable task, and in Rose's state of mind, it was. However, with the help of some professionals, she was able to get through it all.

How much easier all of this would have been if Rose and Tom had done some prior planning and had all their wishes and information gathered in one place, a book, for instance.

Part B — Can We Expect the Unexpected When it Comes to Death?

Sam and Joanne were a young couple in their early 30s, with no children. They both had good jobs and a nice house in an upscale neighborhood. They enjoyed being with each other, had many good friends, traveled, and entertained, and all-in-all, life was good. Then the unexpected happened; Sam was flying to a conference on the West Coast when his plane encountered bad weather and crashed. Sam was not one of the survivors. Joanne was notified of his death and was at a loss about what to do next. The idea of discussing death was something that had not entered their minds. They had too much going for them, and after all, life was good and they were still young, right? Family and friends gathered around and paid their respects, but Joanne had no idea where to begin. Everyone was willing to give her advice and tell her what they would do in her place, but in her shocked state of mind, things just did not make sense, and her confusion just added to her grief. How much easier would things have been had she and Sam made prior plans? At least if Joanne had some place to start, such as with a checklist or if things had been written in a book that was easily accessible, she would not feel quite so lost and alone.

While we all would like to think we will live to old age and die of natural causes, this is not always the case. We can have an undiagnosed medical condition, heart attack, or stroke, or we may be killed in some type of accident, such as with an automobile. For those left behind, these deaths leave survivors in a state of shock, and oftentimes, no preparations have been made regarding even the simple things, such as disposition of the body, not to mention the estate itself. Prior preparations would be invaluable for the survivors. The bottom line is, you are not immortal, and each day is a surprise, no matter how much you plan. No one has a crystal ball that works, so prepare in advance.

Chapter 2
Expected Death

Death will most certainly come to everyone. Sometimes we have a general idea when, as in the case of a disease or illness that we know will result in death. It is also expected that at some point, we will die from "natural causes." For these deaths, you should have your affairs in order by preparing some of the documents discussed in Chapter 4.

A — Death Is No Respecter of Persons or Plans

Beth and Roger married young and raised their two children. The youngest had just started college when Roger was diagnosed with terminal lung cancer. The doctors gave him six to eight months to live. Of course, the first thing Beth and Roger thought was, "It cannot be happening to us; the doctor must be mistaken." Then, the second medical opinion confirmed the first, and Roger started treatments to try to arrest the spread of the cancer and prolong his life. After all, they still had so much to do and wanted to enjoy retirement together after their youngest graduated from college. This was not to be. Instead, they had to start thinking of what needed to be done to prepare Beth to cope with the endless trips to the doctor, the treatments, and in the end, hospice/palliative care. They had not planned for this catastrophe. Roger had no life insurance because they had decided not to buy it in favor of putting that money in the college fund for the kids. The house had been refinanced to also help pay for the college education, so there was a second mortgage. Beth worked as a dental hygienist and knew her salary would not cover the mortgage payments as well as all the other household expenses, car payment, etc. Beth and Roger had to make decisions regarding the house and maintaining the financial stability of Beth when Roger passed on. With such a short time frame to work in, they sought the assistance of a financial planner to determine the best course of action. In addition, both drew up wills and discussed burial plans. This was not what Beth and Roger really wanted to do with the short time remaining, but since it was something they had not talked about before, they were forced into facing reality. Both knew that once Roger reached the hospice/palliative stage, he would not be physically or possibly mentally able to make any decisions. Having to decide about end-of-life care and whether Roger wanted to be resuscitated, if need be, would place a great deal of stress on both at a time when neither was prepared to handle it.

B — Not Related by Blood or Marriage

However different the circumstances, some things remain the same, such as planning, communicating your plans, writing them down, preparing ahead, and acting before it is too late. This is even more important when the relationship between a couple is not considered "legal," i.e., there is no marriage or other contract.

Let us look at Jody and Paul. They have lived together for almost twenty-five years. Jody is 58 and Paul is 63. Paul has a son by a previous marriage. Jody, while married before, has no children. Neither has a will. They do not live in a state that recognizes common law marriage. They both work and pool their resources to pay for household expenses. They jointly own their home. They both have vehicles. What happens if Paul dies before Jody or vice versa? They have worked together to get the things they have, but legally, will Jody inherit Paul's belongings, or will they become the property of his son? Who will make the decision about what happens to Paul if he has made no plans for his death and has told no one what he desires, including Jody? Who prevails — the "significant other," Jody, who has vested a large block of her life into building a life with Paul, or the son, who has his own life and family? Is this a situation that will require the services of a lawyer? Unless the son and Jody can work things out, it could certainly become a very ugly situation. It has been my experience that death changes people. Families are torn apart, arguing over who gets what and how much. No matter how well they got along before the death, after death, all the ugliness comes out, and it becomes a free-for-all regarding dividing property and belongings. If this can happen to a family, related by blood, what do you think will happen when one of the parties is not related at all? The solution is a will or trust that spells out exactly who gets what, but even then, wills may have to be probated and can be contested. Joint ownership of large items, such as real estate and vehicles, may be the only solution, as well as joint bank accounts. If the arrangement throughout the relationship has been one of "separate but equal," then you will find yourself back to square one and hope cooler heads will prevail, but do not count on it. In this case, Jody may find she has next to nothing because Paul's son took the lion's share.

Chapter 3
Planning Ahead

A — Is There Such a Thing as Too Much Planning?

Elizabeth and Jack have been married for fifty-three years and are 74 and 79, respectively. They both retired from careers, she as a schoolteacher and he as a carpenter. During their careers, they aggressively planned for retirement, and as part of that, planned for death. They had life insurance policies, burial policies, wills (including a living will), joint accounts, and a book with information indicating where important papers were located, to include birth certificates, marriage certificates, insurance papers, passports, bank papers, mortgage papers, car titles, etc. All important documents were in a safe deposit box located in their bank. Keys for all vehicles, the house, and the safe deposit box were all labeled, just in case both died together in an accident. They had even planned for the care of their little cocker spaniel, Rex. Jack had served in the U.S. Army during Vietnam, and as a veteran knew he would be entitled to a military burial ceremony and a burial flag.

Instructions to contact the nearest County Veteran Service Counselor were also included in their book. Family (their two sons and a daughter) and close friends knew of the location of this book. They periodically reviewed their insurance plans and their wills to ensure everything was up to date. Nothing was left for their family to have to decide.

Of course, you may say this is a dream situation, but there are those who do plan for any contingency, including death. The most difficult thing about any plan is getting started. It requires frank communication among all parties.

There are many variables in death preparations. If you do not know the location or existence of insurance policies, property documents, bank accounts, retirement funds, etc., the mere task of where to begin finding this information can create a great deal of stress. Once all of these documents are located and in order, consider having an instruction book that will provide this information, such as the one Jack and Elizabeth had compiled.

In the event you are in a position of acting as an executor/executrix/administrator of an estate with no idea where to begin, keep this in mind. Gather all papers in one place and go through them one by one, sorting as you go. You should eventually have a stack of papers that will include bank information, insurance information, etc. Never throw anything out until all affairs of the decedent are settled.

There are some things that we just do not think about. Mary has a friend whose husband was diagnosed with cancer. The treatment was going to be long and costly, not necessarily in terms of money, because he had good insurance, but costly regarding what it would do to his body, his mental health, and the burden it would place on his wife to care for him. There was no guarantee the treatment would work. He decided he did not want to burden his wife, did not want to have his quality of life dissipate and be "helpless," so he committed suicide. There were no warning signs. One day, he got up early, took his pistol and shot himself. His spouse was totally stunned. She had been prepared to stand by his side during treatment and care for him, but his death left her numb. She had no family nearby, and her friends had left town on vacation. She turned to a veterans' counselor for help. In cases like this, it is like taking a child by the hand and gently guiding them down the path, so they will not hurt themselves. Each step was small and sometimes had to be repeated because her thought processes were just not working. Every day brought something new that she had to do or think about. Her husband had taken care of the finances, but thankfully he had started showing her. In addition, he had all his paperwork in order; the mortgage was paid, the bills up to date, etc. Without this prior preparation, the widow would have been faced with an unsurmountable task. Even so, suicide will often negate any insurance policies paying the survivor, so the additional burden of meeting financial obligations comes to the forefront of things that need to be done.

B — Recording Your Wishes

I have mentioned having a book where you keep information such as where all documents are located, where to find keys, whom to notify, and all the other questions that have been brought up, and maybe even some that have not. This book can be a journal, a folder with all the documents, or some other method of keeping information, such as a CD and it should be in a safe deposit box or other secure place. Whatever you use, you need to let someone else know where it is. You could also consider writing a letter to a close relative or friend providing them with instructions regarding your property, where things are located, etc.

C — Keep It Simple

Are you feeling overwhelmed? That would be a natural reaction. In every instance cited in prior scenarios, a prior plan would have made things easier and relieved stress. However, many people are not planners. They live from day to day and put things off until the last minute. They consider planning for an event, such as death, something to be done later, and then when later comes, it is too late. They say, "I'll do it tomorrow." Remember, today is yesterday's tomorrow.

The key to any planning is to keep it simple. This sounds easy, doesn't it? Well, that is not always the case because, as the poet Robert Burns is so often paraphrased, "The best laid plans of mice and men often go awry." However, I am a believer in planning, and sometimes you must play the "what if" game to provide for as many contingencies as possible.

First you start by assuming the inevitable. All of us will die one day. So, if you start with that assumption, you have taken the first step in planning. Some will leave behind relatives and friends, and others will leave behind no one. While it really will not matter to you because you will not be here, it will matter to those you leave behind, and you must decide if you want to make things easier for them. I hope you decide to plan a little.

Even if you do not believe in wills or trusts, a written document of some type will help. A book of your desires, kept in a location where it can be found, will suffice.

Chapter 4
Where Do I Start?

There are many "to-do" books, and there is a plethora of information available on websites. In fact, there is so much information that it is overwhelming. Making plans when you can think about things and organize them will be a lot simpler than trying to figure things out when you are still in shock or grieving after a death.

What should be in your "book"? If you have any of the following documents, your book should provide information regarding locations, etc. Other instructions can also be contained in your book.

A. Wills

How many times have we heard we should have a will? What is a will, and exactly what does it do? A will is a method for us to leave specific instructions in the event of our death. A will spells out exactly what property and belongings there are and to whom it will be left or bequeathed. It eliminates the need for someone to decide where things will go. If you have no will, consider preparing one, as doing so will assist those left behind in the handling of your estate. Some online wills may not be as complete as needed to satisfy all legal requirements. It is often best to contact a lawyer for preparation of a will. After you have prepared a will, be sure you keep this in a safe place (i.e., home safe, bank vault, etc.) and let someone know where it is. Periodically, you should review this document to ensure it is up to date. This is especially important if you marry, divorce, have children, etc. If you have this listed in your book, it will prove to be invaluable in the event of a death. One important aspect of a will is to make sure it is witnessed by at least two people and notarized. Many states will not recognize a written document providing instructions on disposition of your property unless it is witnessed and notarized. Give a copy to a friend or relative and be sure to provide a copy to your executor. If you had your will prepared by a lawyer, they will have a copy in their files, so be sure to indicate in your book what lawyer should be contacted.

B. Living will

OK, so what is the difference between a "will" and a "living will"? A living will is different than the standard will as it provides instructions telling what should be done for health care in the event the individual is no longer able to make those decisions. It is usually done in conjunction with a power of attorney or health care proxy.

Since these are legal documents, they should be witnessed and notarized. Due to their importance, they should be prepared when an individual is still in control of mental faculties. This living will normally covers such things as the course of treatment to be taken by caregivers, sometimes forbidding treatment, and providing instructions about giving food and water in the event the person is unable to give informed consent due to incapacity. The power of attorney or health care proxy appoints an individual who is authorized to direct health care decisions in the event of incapacity of the individual concerned. Many places require a copy of a "do not resuscitate" order to be on file with the local hospital or primary care doctor. You should seek legal help in preparing this document, as with all legal documents. Many places require this document to be signed by a doctor.

C. Trusts

A trust can be set up to ensure your beneficiaries are provided for and are not burdened with expenses involving inheritance taxes and probate. It is a legal arrangement in which your property is managed by a person(s) or an organization for the benefit of someone else, whom you name. You often hear about a trust being set up in the case of a minor child or children. Again, seek legal help to set up a trust.

D. Insurance

(1) Life insurance

There are various types of life insurance policies, and the type you have will determine payout. Most insurance policies require you to name a beneficiary, the person or persons who will get the money upon your death. You should also have a contingent beneficiary or beneficiaries named in the event you and your spouse or significant other perish at the same time. It is important to note that if you are married and then divorced or are married and then the spouse dies, you should change your beneficiary to a different person. The same thing applies when you have one child named as beneficiary, and then have another child or children. Upon death, the insurance company must be notified, and normally they require a death certificate. Contact the insurance company about their procedures since many of them will provide you with the proper forms. Be sure to find out if they need an original of the death certificate, a certified copy, or just a copy. If you have questions regarding the completion of forms for payment, a telephone call or a visit to their website will usually provide you with the information needed. It is important you have your insurance papers located in a safe place, such as a safe deposit box.

(2) Credit cards/financial institutions/mortgage insurance

Many credit cards and financial institutions have insurance policies that will pay off your credit card balance, loan, or mortgage in the event of your death. Information regarding this type of coverage should also be noted in your book and the "policies" kept with your important papers.

(3) Burial insurance

This insurance is normally purchased in advance of death and covers the funeral bills. Check the policy to see what is covered, such as preparation of the body, casket, burial vault, plot, transportation to a different city or state for burial, headstone, etc. Each policy, like life insurance, is different. Funeral homes can assist you with this type of coverage or plan. If you oversee arrangements, be sure you check documents to ascertain what type of coverage the deceased had purchased. Again, this document should be kept with important papers in a safe place. Sometimes this will answer the question regarding disposition of remains, such as whether the person wants burial or cremation or donation of body organs, etc.

E. Financial documents

These documents will be some of the most important because all assets must be accounted for, to include property, vehicles, bank accounts, IRAs, CDs, retirement, disability payments, Social Security, VA disability, and outstanding debts. When accounting for your property, start with the obvious, such as real estate, bank accounts, and vehicles. Then expand your accounting to include the possibility of IRAs, CDs, retirement annuities, disability payments, Social Security payments, VA disability, military retirement, etc.

F. Funeral arrangements

If you do not have burial insurance or a plan with a local funeral home, you should make sure your burial plans are spelled out, and you should specify when and where you want to be buried or cremated and your desires for the disposition of ashes, if cremated. Any specific preferences should be noted, such as ceremony, music, etc. By having this as a separate instruction, you can save the survivors time and stress by having it spelled out. You may also include a list of persons you want notified in the event of your death.

G. Whom to notify

OK, so where do you start? If there were no instructions regarding whom to notify, start with family and friends, those closest to the deceased. You can do this using a phone tree system, the newspaper, or even email. You need to make sure you have all the information people will need, such as date of death, place of death, funeral location and time, flowers or donations, etc. Close friends and family will always ask for the details. In the event you are dealing with a suicide or a homicide as opposed to an accidental or natural death, you may also be dealing with law enforcement authorities. This could delay some of your arrangements, but eventually the result will be the same.

H. Disposition of possessions

Next, it is time to consider all of the deceased's personal property; disposition will be easier if there is a will to specify what to do. However, if there is no will to specify final disposition, you will be left with determining how to dispose of the property. Generally, in the case of no will, the estate will go into probate. This means there will be an accounting made of all disposition of property to the Probate Court. If there are family members, the court must decide what to do with possessions. This can always be a very problematic area, especially if the family does not get along or if the possessions left have high value. There is no easy solution to this problem, other than trying to come to an agreement on who gets what. If there is no family, then friends must make these same decisions. There are many charities and other organizations that will gladly accept your donations. You will need to contact each organization to determine what they will and will not take as donations.

(1) Joint accounts

Most joint accounts have incorporated into them an agreement, usually referred to as a "right of survivorship" or a "POD" (pay on death) clause. This is an especially important clause, and whenever you are establishing joint accounts, you need to know what the written agreement entails. In most cases, such as with bank accounts, you will have to present a death certificate to show the account holder is deceased and then work with the bank or other financial entity to determine proper disposition of the holding, such as having it transferred to another account, closing the account, etc.

(2) Vehicles (to include boats, RV's, motorcycles, etc.)

Are the vehicles titled or registered in only one name? If so, then the disposition of this property should be addressed in a will. If there is no will, legal right of ownership will have to be established. The result in either case will be having the car titled in the survivor's name. If there is a lien on the vehicle, the loan will have to be resolved first. This could either mean refinancing in the survivor's name or having the vehicle sold to pay off the loan. You will need to work with the finance institution on this agreement. In addition, you will need to go to the DMV in the area where the deceased lived or had the vehicles registered to change titles to a different owner.

(3) Real estate

Again, this should be covered in a will. If the home was purchased with two people on the mortgage, the second person should inherit via "right of survivorship." If there is insurance that pays off the home in the event of death, this should be indicated in the decedent's planning book. You will need to contact the mortgage holder for information regarding how to proceed. If there is only one person on the mortgage, the deceased, this again becomes a matter for a legal resolution. If the property is in joint ownership by two people who are not married, this can be resolved via a legal document that will ensure the property is inherited by the survivor and thus can be kept out of probate proceedings.

The determination of how to dispose of property and personal belongings may be made by the Probate Court with no idea what the deceased may have wanted.

Chapter 5

Things To Consider During Planning Or Upon Death

A. Obituary

If you have set up burial arrangements with a funeral home, you can also write your own obituary. If not, they can often help. You need to be careful regarding the information you include due to identity theft.

B. Social Security

You will need to notify the Social Security Administration. Often this is automatic when the death is reported. However, if not, it will most likely be done by going to the local Social Security office. You will need a death certificate and any probate papers as well as the Social Security number and vital information of the deceased.

C. Credit reporting agencies

The three credit reporting agencies should be notified of death. This can normally be done by a phone call. Mail copies of the death certificate to all three credit-reporting bureaus, Equifax, Experian, and TransUnion, and to any credit issuers who require one to cancel accounts right after the person dies. A few weeks after taking these steps, you may want to run a credit report on the deceased just to ensure there has been no activity. You can get a free report from each bureau at www.annualcreditreport.com (check to make sure this is a free one).

D. Miscellaneous information

If you are going through probate, the clerk of the court will provide you with guidance as to what reports you will need to file and any other requirements. You will be responsible for safeguarding the estate's assets and as such will be accountable for preparing and filing all required reports and paying all debts. If you are the administrator of a will, you will need to distribute the estate's assets in accordance with the will. Keep in mind if there is no will, you will most likely have to get bonded as well as work through the probate clerk. All these things cost money. Be prepared. If you are the executor, you may have to establish an "estate account" where all monies will be deposited, and all bills will be paid from the account. Each state has its own laws concerning this.

If your bank accounts, car, house, stocks, and other property are in JOINT TENANCY, WITH RIGHT OF SURVIVOR, these accounts can be transferred to the survivor's name with the presentation of a death certificate and proof of identity. There may be some forms to fill out. However, under joint tenancy, the account/assets automatically transfer to the survivor upon the death of the joint owner. This transfer does not go through the probate courts.

Collect and identify all the keys/combinations for the real property, the vehicles, and the safe deposit boxes. When planning, you can make sure all keys are labeled and their location is known to survivors.

You will need to know passwords on accounts, ATM cards, etc., because as we all know, everything needs a password. This is information that would be important to keep in your planning book. This can save time when trying to close out accounts that contain asset information.

Sort paperwork according to things like financial institutions, credit cards, insurance policies, etc. Place them in separate boxes for examination later.

Contact the Department of Motor Vehicles to cancel any driver's license to prevent a duplicate from being issued.

E. Death certificates

You will normally need a minimum of ten copies of the certified death certificate. Some entities will accept a copy of the death certificate, but others will require a certified copy. You will have to check with each place to determine what is acceptable. If you need additional certified copies, the funeral home that handled arrangements can assist.

F. Other considerations

If payments from retirement sources or disability are direct deposit, be sure to leave the money in the accounts. Normally upon notification to the organizations who are paying the benefit, they will recover any funds due and issue those that still need to be paid. Because of this, it is important to keep accounts open until after this has been accomplished.

Chapter 6

Getting Through The Inevitable

So now you have been told that your loved one is dying. How do you handle this? How can you possibly even think things will be normal again? Some turn to their religion for strength, some to friends, some family. Whatever you use, you know it will not prevent the final resulting death. The Buddhists have a philosophy that says to help the person who is dying they sit with them and tell them stories of happy things, sharing with them memories that evoke pleasant thoughts to help take their mind off their pain and dying so that they can pass peacefully.

WALK WITHIN YOU

If I be the first of us to die,
Let grief not blacken long your sky,
Be bold yet modest in your grieving.
There is a change but not a leaving.
For just as death is part of life,
The dead live on forever in the living.
What we were, we are.
What we had, we have,
A conjoined past imperishably present.

So, when you walk the woods where once we
walked together
And scan in vain the dappled bank beside you for my shadow
Or pause where we always did upon the hill to gaze
across the land,
And spotting something, reach by habit for my hand,
And finding none, feel sorrow start to steal upon you,
Be still. Close your eyes. Breathe.
Listen for my footfall in your heart.
I am not gone but merely walk within you.

From Nicholas Evans, *The Smoke Jumper*

Chapter 7
Do I Need A Lawyer?

This is always a good idea in order to protect yourself and ensure all legalities are followed. Some of these situations will best be legally accomplished by a lawyer. They may include situations such as no will, Probate Court, wrongful death, business holdings, and family members who may contest a will if there is one or come for "their share" if there is not. A lawyer will assist you in negotiating all the legal hurdles and provide protection for you.

Chapter 8
Special Circumstances

Many family members have a history of either having served in the military or being retired from the military. There are special things to remember in these cases.

If you happen to be in the Armed Forces, there is a whole new set of rules. The good thing is most services have what is called "decedent affairs," which means they normally have an office that handles deaths. That is the good news. The not-so-good news is that you still must have plans and have some type of idea of what to do, where to go, and whom to talk to. Usually, the personnel office can assist in this. As a military member, it is your responsibility to ensure all your documents, such as the "Record of Emergency Data," are up to date. This means making sure any changes in your status, i.e., marriage, divorce, children, etc., are provided for in periodic updates and reviews.

Chapter 9
One Last Thing: A Personal Letter

There is a suggestion that as part of your estate plan, you should write a letter to those you leave behind. In the letter you can write what is in your heart. Tell them what they have meant to you, and that you love them and are proud of them. Mention treasured moments you spent with them in childhood, as a family member or friend. If there are those you feel you have hurt, tell them you are sorry, and forgive those who may have hurt you. Thank those you love and who have cared for you and say goodbye. This is a way to help survivors through the grieving process.

MEMORIES

Everyone has them.
They are uniquely yours.
No one can take them away.
You cannot give yours to anyone.
You can share them.
You can make new ones.
They cannot be destroyed by fire or flood
Or lost in a move or taken away by a divorce.

Only death will stop your memories from accumulating
and being relived.
Every event makes new memories and sometimes renews
old memories.
But each person remembers the event a little differently.
That is why your memories are unique to you.
So, treasure your memories.

They are snapshots stored in your brain
And whenever you want to retrieve them
All you must do is think about something
And there they are.
Whatever memories you have will be.
The only thing you can take with you when you die.
You cannot take family or friends,
You cannot take happiness or heartbreak, only the
memories of each,
Because all else disappears with death.
Your memories will remain
Locked forever in your brain
When death overtakes you,
Like closing a book after you read the last word of the last
page of the last chapter.

Chapter 10
The Grieving Process

It will not matter if the death was expected or unexpected; the survivor(s) will go through a grieving process. Each person will handle death in a different manner, but most will go through the various stages of grief, which are shock and disbelief, blame, anger, bargaining, depression, and acceptance. You may not go through all the stages; you may skip some and then come back later. While people will tell you that they know how you are feeling, they really do not unless you verbalize how you feel.

It is important you recognize the fact that you may be in one of these stages and that moving through them will finally bring you to acceptance and some peace. Many survivors think something is wrong with them because they are not able to function either mentally, physically, or both. One widow described it as "fuzzy brain." They replay the death over and over in their minds, thinking there must have been something they did or did not do or something they could have done better, until they totally debilitate themselves. This is when it is important to seek counseling, either through private sources or through bereavement groups. Bereavement groups can provide you with support from those who have gone through the same thing and can best identify with your dilemma. There is nothing wrong with seeking help through these groups.

The first hurdle after shock and disbelief is facing the fact you may now be living alone in the same place you shared with your loved one. In the beginning, there is a lot of activity, such as friends and family coming and going, many details to take care of, etc. However, there will come a time when you will be left alone to face the silence, to know you cannot have a two-way conversation with your loved one, to know they will not be there when you come home or turn around. The first time this happens will be one of the hardest times you will face.

Thoughts will creep into your mind, such as the idea that this must be a dream, this could not be happening, or this is all wrong. The reality of the situation has not permeated the depth of your soul. There may be activity, however mind numbing, and people around you, but you are not fully cognizant of what is going on. You are in a dream state, suspended in time but not in reality. You may even withdraw from those you were close to prior to the death because they only bring pain. Eventually, they will return to their lives and you must return to your new life, a life with a missing piece.

You will relive the last hours, days, and minutes of your loved one's passing. You will cry, laugh, shout, and maybe even curse. How could this be? What went wrong? Did I do everything I could have done? Whose fault is this?

What will I do now? Where will I go? You are angry with yourself, with your friends, and with the world around you. You are angry because this happened, and you had no control. Unfortunately, you will have to face this time, and the way through will be up to you. Some things you will have to do by rote, just numbly going through the daily process of living, cooking, cleaning, washing clothes, washing dishes, going back to work, getting outside, and finally learning how to do things by yourself. You will have to come to grips with a new life, a life after death.

This can be especially trying for those who must have control of their lives and the things around them. Letting go will be even more difficult for them. Then there is blame — blame for others and blame for yourself. The doctor should have found this sooner; I should have done something differently; "if only." Getting through this stage requires you to finally face the fact there was really nothing you could have done. You must understand there are just some things in life over which you will have no control. You will be a spectator and not an active participant. When you can accept this concept, you can then move on and take control over those things in your life that you need.

For some there is bargaining. For people who are religious, this can mean bargaining through prayer. If I change my life, will he take this back? Will he make it all go away? I know it is a dream. I promise to change the way I do things if only I can shut my eyes and when I open them again, everything will be ok.

Despair and depression can take over your life. You cannot function; you have no desire to do anything. You do not want to move; even eating is a chore. You may realize you have to go back to work or do something to keep busy so you do not have to think, and by doing this, perhaps the drive to live returns. Keeping busy is important because it keeps your brain stimulated and allows you to begin to cope with life after death.

Finally, there is acceptance. You can finally accept the reality of your loss. Even in acceptance, you may find some of the other stages creep in, such as anger and depression. You may never fully "forget," especially if the relationship was a long and loving one. You will eventually find peace — peace in knowing you have wonderful memories that can never be taken away. You will move on to make a life for yourself, and it may always contain these memories, but they will not consume you to the point of incapacitation. This, then, is what life after death is all about — when you come to realize that life does, in fact, go on and you are still alive, and you have choices to make. You can choose to live your life knowing you had the time with your loved one, or you can choose to hate your existence. Should you choose the latter, you may find you need to seek some outside help to get you through this period and to move onto a different plane.

Know yourself and allow yourself to live again. Let your feelings ebb and flow; cry, shout, and do whatever you need to do to go on with life, because you know this is what your loved one would really want you to do, and if the roles were reversed, this is what you would want them to do.

Can one ever be fully prepared for death? I am not sure. Perhaps those very enlightened individuals who are spiritually in touch with the all-powerful can, and then again, perhaps they cannot. The bottom line is, we will all perish one day, and it will be easier for those we have left behind if we help prepare them to go on living. Prepare for LIFE AFTER DEATH.

> You can shed tears that she is gone,
> or you can smile because she has lived.
> You can close your eyes and pray that she'll come back,
> or you can open your eyes and see all she's left.
> Your heart can be empty because you can't see her,
> or you can be full of the love you shared.
> You can turn your back on tomorrow and live yesterday,
> or you can be happy for tomorrow because of yesterday.
> You can remember her only that she is gone,
> or you can cherish her memory and let it live on.
> You can cry and close your mind,
> Be empty and turn your back.
> Or you can do what she'd want:
> Smile, open your eyes, love and go on."

David Harkins

Chapter 11
The Final Chapter

No matter what your walk in life is, no matter how much you prepare, Death is no respecter of persons. We will all face the death of a loved one or friend one day, and how we cope with this death is hidden deep inside each of us. Having a plan in place to get you through the "paperwork" and allow you to move out the other side can become essential to your wellbeing and relieve some of the stress you will experience.

Chapter 12
Recap

Here is a checklist of things you will need to accomplish upon planning for or dealing with a death. Some have already been addressed in previous chapters, so this is just a quick overview.

Preparations—checklist
    a. Will
    b. Funeral/cremation*
    c. Insurance
    d. Financial
    e. Credit cards
    f. Driver's license
    g. Professional organizations
    h. Mail
    i. Newspaper/magazines
    j. Military notification
    k. Veterans Administration
    l. Pension plans
    m. IRA/CD
    n. Bank
    o. Vehicle registration/insurance

p. Social Security
q. Mortgage company
r. Credit bureaus
s. Loans
t. Cancel pending doctor appointments
u. Clubs and organizations
v. IRS, property tax

Disposition of possessions
    a. Established by will
    b. No will
    c. Donate

Grieving process
    a. Stages
    b. Support groups

*NOTE: Check to see if any insurance policy exists which has prepaid burial or cremation, to include plot and services.

First, gather all paperwork, bills, documents, etc. together and sort them according to type. To do this, get some boxes, and as you sort, put like documents in a box. In this way, you can go through them later, and it will also be easier to determine which documents may be more important than others.

Insurance: Did the deceased have any life insurance, mortgage, car, or credit card insurance, etc.? Begin with life insurance because insurance companies need to be notified for payment purposes. Each insurance company has its own set of procedures. Check the policy to determine whom to contact and what documents are required. Usually, a copy of the death certificate will be needed.

Credit cards and banks have insurance policies that cover paying off the balance, loan, or mortgage in the event of death. Information regarding this type of coverage would be available either through documentation or direct contact with the company, bank, or mortgage company.

Financial: Account for all assets. Start with the obvious, such as property, bank accounts, and vehicles. Then explore the possibility of IRAs, CDs, retirement annuities, disability payments, Social Security payments, VA disability, military retirement, etc.

Credit cards: Contact the credit card companies and let them know of the death. If you are listed as a user, be sure to let the company know. Some companies will require you to reapply for the card in your name only. Contact the credit reporting agencies so no one will be able to utilize the deceased person's information.

IRS/CDs/stocks/bonds: Many people have a financial portfolio or even a financial advisor who has all this information. Sometimes, the bank is the best source of information.

Vehicle registration/insurance: If vehicle is paid for, there should be a title. The title will most likely need to be changed to remove the deceased. Some titles are available online and require a payment to print out a paper copy. In addition, notify the car insurance company.

Social Security: If you have internet access, go to www.ssa.gov. You can report a death by calling the 800 number on business days. Be sure to have the deceased's Social Security number available. If you are a surviving spouse, you could be entitled to a $255 death benefit and can obtain additional information regarding filing from the Social Security office. This may require an in-person visit. They will most likely require a certified copy of your birth certificate, as well as the deceased's, and a picture ID, a certified copy of your marriage certificate (if applicable), and a certified copy of the death certificate.

Professional organizations/mail/newspapers and magazines: Be sure to notify each of these in the event of death.

Military/Veterans Administration/pension plans: Check to make sure these three entities are notified of death.

Mortgage company: If real estate is involved, contact the mortgage company.

Joint accounts: If you have joint accounts, there should have been some type of "right of survivorship" agreement.

This is especially important in joint accounts. For your planning, be sure to check with your bank or credit union to ensure proper documents are prepared and on file.

Credit bureaus: Notify the three credit bureaus, TransUnion, Experian, and Equifax, so no one can utilize deceased identification.

Miscellaneous: Cancel any medical/dental appointments.

Disposition of possessions: A will determines how to dispose of possessions. If there is no will, disposition will be a personal matter regarding what possessions you sell or donate and which you keep. You may need to work through a Probate Court to meet legal requirements.

Grieving: It will not matter if the death was expected or unexpected; the survivor will go through a grieving process. Each person will handle death in a different manner, but most will go through various stages of grief, such as shock, disbelief, blame, anger, and finally acceptance.
    Many organizations have groups available to provide support in your time of need.
    Know yourself and allow yourself to live again. Let your feelings ebb and flow; cry, shout and do what your loved one would really want you to do and, if the roles were reversed, what you would want them to do. This could be the end, or it may be the start of a new beginning; it's your choice.

Chapter 13
Reflections

"They that love beyond the world cannot be separated by it. ... Death is but crossing the world, as friends do the seas; they live in one another still."
— William Penn

THE WATCH

For twenty years
This sailor has stood the watch
While some of us were in school learning our trade
This shipmate stood the watch
Yes. Even before some of us were born into this world
This shipmate stood the watch
In those years when the storm clouds of war were seen brewing on the horizon of history
This shipmate stood the watch
Many times he would cast an eye ashore and see his family standing there
Needing his guidance and help

Needing that hand to hold during those hard times
But he still stood the watch
He stood the watch for twenty years
He stood the watch so that we, our families and
Our fellow countrymen could sleep soundly in safety
Each and every night
Knowing that a sailor stood the watch
Today we are here to say
"Shipmate … the watch stands relieved
Relieved by those you have trained, guided and led
Shipmate you stand relieved … We have the watch …

"Boatswain. Standby to pipe the side … Shipmate's going Ashore."

— William Whiting, 1860

Addendum

I hope this little book has been of some assistance in planning for this life event.

The following is what I personally went through when my brother, Charlie, died. Although he had COPD, this was not an expected event when it happened. I knew sometime in the future I would have to face this, but I was not prepared for this day. While he was a highly organized person, there were still many details that I had to work out, and I had only myself to accomplish this task.

Charlie had started preparation for his burial but never completed them. The only part done was arrangements for burial in a Veterans Administration cemetery. I had a handwritten will that was not witnessed or notarized. The court said it was like having no will, and I had to go to probate. This meant hiring a lawyer and getting bonded. Those two things had to happen before I could go before the probate clerk to have them determine if the estate was mine. Since I was the sole heir, it was straightforward. I had to have both my lawyer and the bondsman present at my meeting with the probate clerk. If there had been any other survivors, such as spouse, children, etc., it would have been a longer process, as all parties would have to be represented. It was still a process, and I had no clue where to start. Four days before I was due to depart the state and return home, I found Charlie's signed, witnessed, and notarized will with some totally unrelated papers in a folder marked "Old Funeral Arrangements." He had another file marked "Funeral Arrangements," which turned out to be incomplete regarding disposition of remains. I had to deal with property taxes, house insurance, disposition of vehicles that did not run, changing titles of vehicles to my name, notifying credit cards, medical insurance, Social Security, the driver's license bureau, mail forwarding, donation of personal items, clearing the house for listing, real estate agents and contracts, returning medical devices that were on loan, destruction of medications, and many other small details. I had to get a roll-off dumpster to throw away all the stuff that was unusable. I had boxes of papers to go through as he had kept all his receipts and income tax stuff from 1988 to 2018. I had to go through each file of papers and look in all drawers and containers because he had a habit of sticking money in things. Also, my mother had lived with him prior to her death in 2015, and he still had her belongings, and she also would stuff money in things. I had to pick and choose what I wanted to keep, what I wanted to give to people, and what was donatable or trash. It took me over five weeks to go through everything, and then I felt I had only scratched the surface. It was good that I was retired and had the time to do this, because had I been working, I would not have been able to spend so much time. Without the help of some of the people who knew him, I would have been walking around in the dark. So just be aware that you may face all types of situations. There were things that came up a year after his death, such as filing income tax on the estate and determining if he had needed to file an income tax return, a call from the VA because they could not close out their file without a death certificate, which I had sent but apparently not to the right department, and personal property tax every six months on the two vehicles that were on the lot for sale but had not sold. In addition, the bond company had to have a copy of the final probate report to close their files or I would have had to pay another bond fee. Nothing was said about this at the time of the bonding. This is where legal advice and a good tax accountant came in handy. Keep in mind, all these things cost money — money that must be paid up front. Dealing long distance with selling a house is a nightmare. I had to have inspections of the property, the dwelling, the well, and the septic tank. Again, all these things cost money. I had a good real estate agent who arranged for these inspections, but it was a back-and-forth process, and then came the offers, many of which were people just trying to take advantage. Thank goodness for email and the use of computers. It meant I did not have to be there in person to sign paperwork, etc. I hired a property manager to oversee the property and ensure the heat was regulated over the winter months. The bottom line to all these things is I never had the time to fully grieve the loss of my brother until almost a year later. One day, as I was sitting looking outside my window, it hit me like a ton of bricks. This is another downside to dealing with death, the aftermath, the life after death.

In contrast, when my mother died, my brother, who was still alive at the time, and I found she had arranged for everything to include transportation from Virginia to Missouri, where she had arranged for burial with the rest of her family. She had everything paid for, including the funeral home, casket, etc. She had left instructions on the music, where she was to be buried, and who she wanted in attendance. My brother and I only had to show up for the ceremony and attend to family who came. It made it quite easy and certainly less stressful.

As you can see, although some things in death can be the same, each death is a little different, and events surrounding the death are all unique. No matter what, the bottom line is you can never be too prepared or in some cases prepared at all for death, be it your own or someone else's, because there will always be LIFE AFTER DEATH.

www.ingramcontent.com/pod-product-compliance
Lightning Source LLC
LaVergne TN
LVHW021735060526
838200LV00052B/3287